Praise for Lisa Bogart

Leave it to Lisa Bogart to come up with a project that soothes the body, feeds the soul, and stimulates the creative heart.

Debbie Macomber, #1 *New York Times* best-selling author

Studies have shown that coloring relaxes us and puts us in a meditative spot. Combine coloring with devotionals and you not only have a bright idea, but a wonderful way to ponder and deepen our relationship with God while we color. This is a wonderful coloring book devotional that will feed your creativity while inspiring your heart and mind.

Georgia Shaffer, author of *Avoiding the 12 Relationship Mistakes Women Make*, Christian life coach, and PA licensed psychologist

As a Christian counselor and coach, I always knew how therapeutic art could be, but I never actually experienced it until recently when I picked up my pens and paints and started to draw and paint. Lisa's book not only provides great thoughts to ponder, but she also creates pages for you to color. Try it. It's not only fun and releases stress, it actually helps you remember what you just read.

Leslie Vernick, licensed counselor, relationship coach, and author of seven books, including *The Emotionally Destructive Relationship* and *The Emotionally Destructive Marriage*

Add crayons and colored pencils to your tools of praise! If Lisa Bogart had just written a book of meditations on quotes from Charles Schulz, Madeleine L'Engle, and reflections on verses of scripture and classic hymns, her musings would be more than enough to commend her joyous new book. But Lisa goes where no devotional book has gone before. She also created a full page of art as a companion to each entry. Lisa's art is delightfully refreshing, surprising in its variety, and explosive in its exuberance. So inspiring!

C. McNair Wilson, author/speaker *HATCH!: Brainstorming Secrets of a Theme Park Designer*

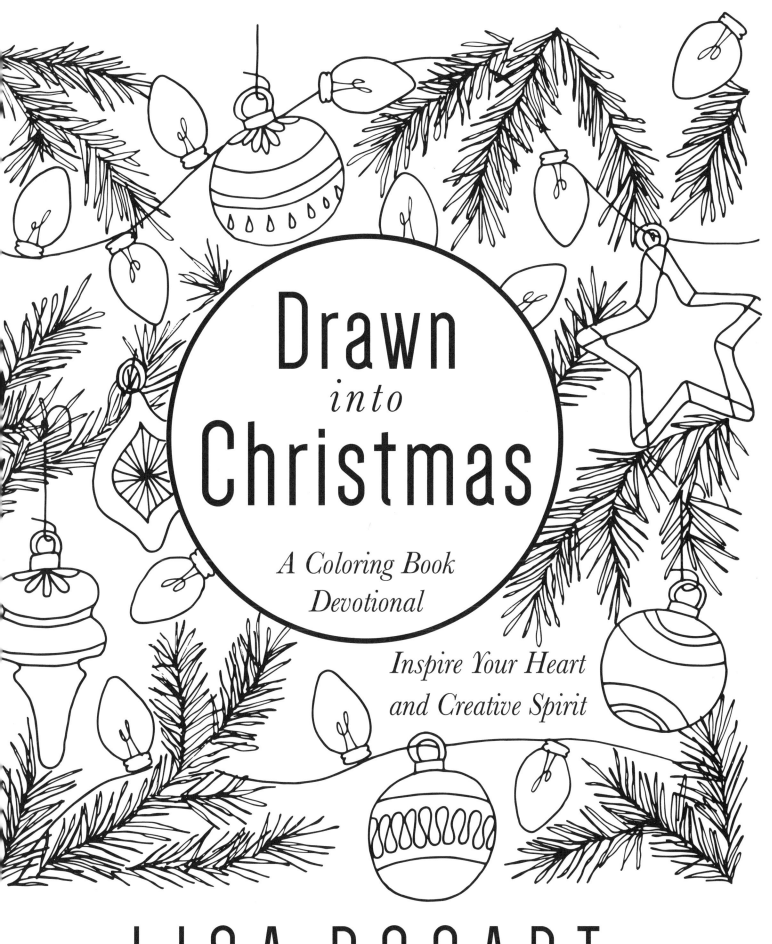

Drawn into Christmas

A Coloring Book
Devotional

Inspire Your Heart
and Creative Spirit

LISA BOGART

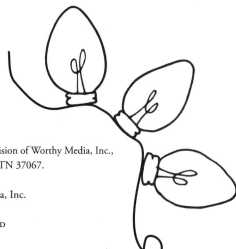

Published by Worthy Inspired, an imprint of Worthy Publishing Group, a division of Worthy Media, Inc.,
One Franklin Park, 6100 Tower Circle, Suite 210, Franklin, TN 37067.

WORTHY is a registered trademark of Worthy Media, Inc.

HELPING PEOPLE EXPERIENCE THE HEART OF GOD

Library of Congress Control Number: 2016947146

ISBN: 978-1-61795-734-5

For foreign and subsidiary rights, contact rights@worthypublishing.com.

Cover Design: Jeff Jansen / Aesthetic Soup
Cover and Interior Illustrations: Lisa Bogart

Printed in the United States of America

16 17 18 19 20 21 RRD 11 10 9 8 7 6 5 4 3 2 1

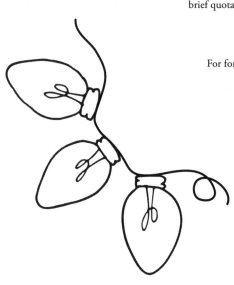

Contents

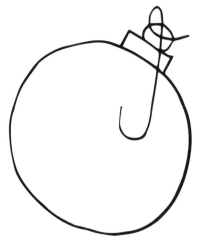

Merry Christmas

'Tis the season to slow down and color. Seriously. Do you remember coloring as a kid at Christmastime? I do. I drew pages of Santas and Christmas trees and bells and ornaments and stockings. I have cut out more than my fair share of snowflakes. And I've made yards of paper chains. Arts and crafts are entwined with the holiday for me.

I want to share my enthusiasm for coloring with you. I know it's a very busy time of year; from shopping to celebrating, your to-do list gets longer each day. The thought of taking a moment to play may seem like a waste of time right now. Let me suggest it would be a terrific use of your time. Take a break from your holiday list of needs-to-get-done-right-now and relax for half an hour. Read a devotion, color a page, and reflect on what we are celebrating, the birth of our Savior.

Christmas is a nostalgic time and definitely a time for children. Allow yourself to have some childlike fun with some grown-up insights. Treat yourself. It will not be a waste of time. It will make you smile.

Pass Along the Message

Said the night wind to the little lamb,
"Do you see what I see?"
Noel Regney

Have you ever played the party game Telephone? The first person whispers a message to their neighbor, but only one time, not repeating a word. That person in turn whispers what he heard to his neighbor, once, no repeating. And so on and so on around the room till the person at the end speaks the message aloud for all to hear. Something is usually lost in translation with hilarious results. *He's making a list and checking it twice.* Comes out the other end: *He's baking a list of chicken and rice.*

Telephone is a funny party game and offers giggles all around. But what if the information being passed along is critical, even life-changing? You'd want to be sure to get the message correct.

I've always thought of the Christmas tune "Do You Hear What I Hear?" as a game of Telephone. The message seems to start from the very heart of God with nature itself. It's the wind that whispers to the little lamb about a star. The lamb tells the shepherd about a song. The shepherd informs the king about the Christ child. And the king implores the people to pray for peace and the child bringing goodness. This is the best game of Telephone EVER. Each participant adds to the message; they don't distort it.

I discovered that this song was originally written in the fall of 1962 during the Cuban Missile Crisis. At the time Americans thought the Soviet Union had nuclear bombs in Cuba ready to launch an attack on the United States. "Do You Hear What I Hear?" was written as a plea for peace during a time of great fear. It sold over 250,000 copies that first Christmas season. It has since been recorded by hundreds of artists and sold tens of millions of copies. The good news of the message still rings out loud and clear: Christ will bring peace to the world.

We are celebrating the birth of our Savior. That is news worth sharing with others. Nothing seems to get lost in the translation; it is still a message of love.

Thank You for the message of Christ's birth reaching all the way to my ear.
I am eager to share the good news.
Amen

SAID THE NIGHT WIND
TO THE LITTLE LAMB
DO YOU SEE WHAT I SEE?

A STAR DANCING IN THE NIGHT
WITH A TAIL AS BIG AS A KITE.

Ringing Together

I heard the bells on Christmas Day,
Their old familiar carols play,
And wild and sweet the words repeat,
Of peace on earth, good will to men.

Henry Wadsworth Longfellow

love ringing handbells. I hated to leave the handbell choir when we moved. Our new church had bells, but not an active handbell choir. When the music director planned special handbell music for Christmas, I eagerly signed up to play. But there weren't enough hands to cover three octaves of bells. We needed more players to pull this off.

I asked my son if he'd be interested. He played clarinet in the junior high band, and reading music was the only requirement to ring bells. As you can imagine, playing in a handbell choir with your mom was not exactly a thrill for a teenager, but Zach said he'd try. He took to it immediately and enjoyed the challenge.

Zach and I stood side by side at the treble end of the bell table. We both played two bells in each hand, so between the two of us we covered an entire octave.

The little impromptu Christmas handbell choir was pretty good, so he asked if we would play again at Easter. Everyone agreed and soon we played throughout the year.

Zach's favor to me had resulted in a five-year commitment to our handbell choir. I knew his senior year of high school would be his last year in the choir. I was sad. I'd miss our Monday night rehearsals. I loved just standing next to Zach. He was a good musician and helped me when I had trouble with complicated rhythms. And sometimes the ride to and from rehearsal was the perfect time to talk. He'd occasionally share thoughts and feelings about his day in the quiet of the car that I'd never hear over the dinner table. I knew I'd miss that alone time even more than playing bells together.

That Christmas I looked out at the congregation. I saw toddlers squirming on laps and smiled. Those days were long gone for me and Zach. I glanced at my son towering next to me. Not a hand held kid anymore, nearly a grown man. I was going to miss him.

I looked out at the congregation again. This time I spotted a few young adults home from college happily sitting next to parents and siblings. I smiled. Zach would be back. But it would be different, as we would not be making music side by side anymore.

As I began to play, the music comforted me. It didn't matter that Zach would be gone next year. He was here now. We were enjoying this moment together. And the tunes would ring in my head long after the bells were packed away in their cases.

Thank You for the memories of Christmas past.
For the music we hold dear and the dear ones who make music with us,
singing, ringing, or just humming along.
Amen

October Christmas

I love Christmas decorations. I like pulling them out each year, remembering when and where I bought them. I like decking the halls of my home and putting lights on the house. I usually do all this in December. Retailers, however, seem to think Christmas begins in September. I grumble like Scrooge when I see nutcrackers and tinsel displayed next to the Halloween candy. Still, now that I live closer to New York City it is fun to go in and see the city sparkling with holiday cheer. It really does put me in a festive mood.

Walking up Fifth Avenue past all the shop windows is a treat. Saks. Bergdorf Goodman. Tiffany's. People literally line up to walk past the window displays. It is fun to see a whole story unfold in each tableau.

Most of the Manhattan decorations seem over the top. The nutcrackers on the street across from Radio City Music Hall are nearly a story tall. There are giant Christmas ornaments, wreaths, and lights blinking on store after store. Grand Central Station is glittering with garland inside and out. The Empire State Building is lit up in red and green most nights. And, of course, there is the enormous tree beside the skating rink at Rockefeller Center. Everything is oversized and wonderful. And while I love it, all these things start appearing in late October to early November. It can make me feel like I'm behind on my holiday to-do list before I've even written it!

So I decided to embrace it. After all, I have been known to hum Christmas tunes in July. And I found a great line buried at the end of the song "It's Beginning to Look a Lot Like Christmas." The last lovely thought is that the thing that makes the season ring is the carol that you sing right within your heart.

Yes, retail Christmas comes out early each year, and yes, it makes us weary. But the joy of Christmas is a great thing. This year, when you see your first Christmas decoration in October, think of it as a chance to bring the joy into your heart right now. Be reminded of what Christmas really means: Jesus was born. Peace on earth, goodwill to men. That is a sentiment you can use all year long. It's beginning to look a lot like love.

Happy Halloween and Merry Christmas.
Even as holidays collide in the stores, let me have joy in my heart this Christmas.
Amen

IT'S BEGIN-
NING TO LOOK
A LOT LIKE
CHRISTMAS

Sugar Cookies

For when the way is rough, your patience has a chance to grow.
So let it grow and don't try to squirm out of your problems.
For when your patience is finally in full bloom, then you will be ready for anything,
strong in character, full and complete.

James 1:3-4 TLB

I hate character-building experiences. Mostly because at the time I do not know I'm building character. At the time I am frustrated and annoyed, or worse, downtrodden and beaten. In big ways and small I've had lots of chances to grow my patience. But I try to squirm out of those situations. Cleaning my room as a kid. Applying to colleges as a teenager. Balancing my checkbook as an adult. All times I wanted to run and hide.

I fake patience most of the time, meaning I am calm in a challenge for a little bit and then I need things to go smoothly. Here's a little challenge: baking sugar cookies for the holiday. Our family recipe is delicious but challenging. Delicious, even though it has sour cream in it (I'm not a fan). But challenging because the dough is very sticky and hard to roll out. These cookies require pluck, grit, and patience. See paragraph one: I lack all of those things.

I try to stay calm while making sugar cookies each Christmas, but some years I fail. I want to be good at taking my time and using enough flour to dust everything so it won't stick to the counter, or the rolling pin, or my fingers. But sometimes the dough and I do not get along. I get frustrated too soon. One year the whole thing ended up in the trash. No homemade cookies at all, store-bought only. Sigh.

Okay, so rolling out sugar cookies is a rather tiny character-building experience. But hear me out. Any little test helps strengthen the muscle. Learning with the small things is much easier than being asked for immediate patience with a large problem.

If you can learn patience from the just annoying times, then the skill is ready when you are hit with a big disappointment. Patience is hard, and there is no way to rush it. And so practicing with something as simple as sugar cookies is a good idea. Besides, you get such a delicious result. Even if they are not lovely shapes, they will taste good. And you can put frosting on anything to improve it 100 percent!

Rough times build my patience. Help me remember the lessons
so they sink into my nature and make me strong in character.
Amen

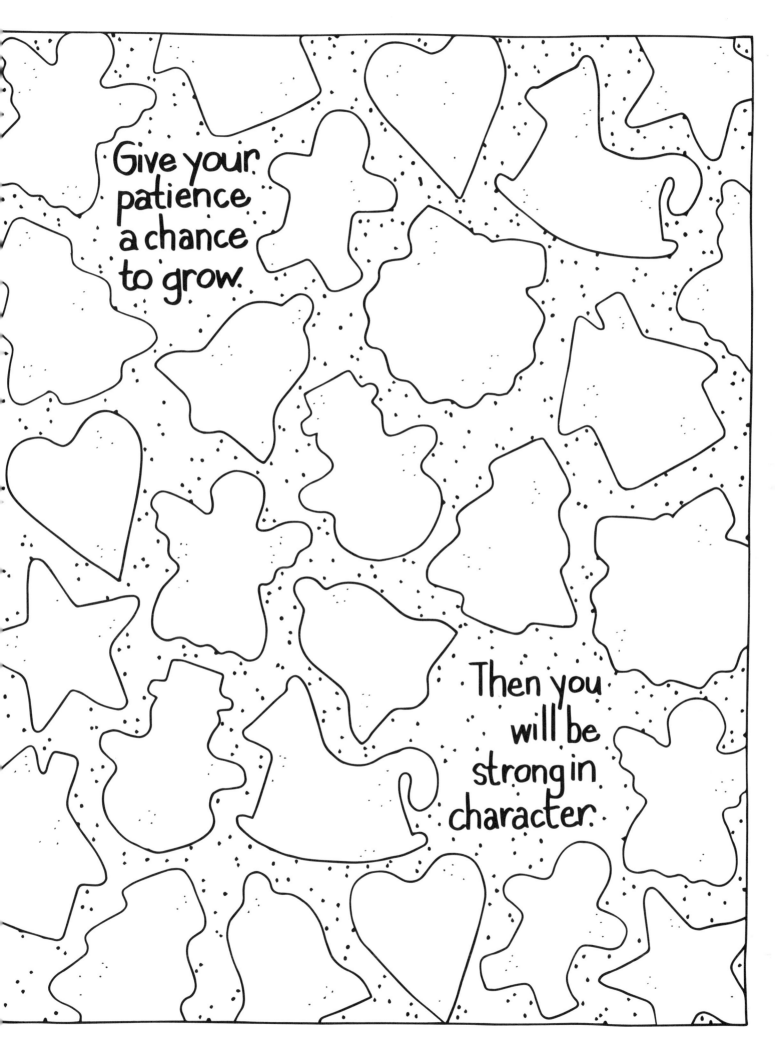

Give your patience a chance to grow.

Then you will be strong in character.

Sugar Cookie Recipe

C is for cookie. That's good enough for me.
Cookie Monster

I suspect that when you were reading about the challenge of my family's sugar cookie recipe, some of you were thinking, *How hard can it be?* Well, I am happy to share the recipe with you so you can find out. It is not that hard, honest. But patience is required. Just remembering to make the dough ahead of time can be a challenge. It really does have to be very cold to work well. Let it sit in the fridge overnight. One trick to speed up the process is to make the dough into four or five smaller balls and then put it in the fridge. Then it only takes an hour or two for it to chill. Good luck!

⅓ cup butter

⅓ cup shortening (Crisco)

¾ cup sugar

1 egg

2 teaspoons vanilla

2 cups flour

½ teaspoon baking soda

½ teaspoon salt

1 teaspoon baking powder

½ cup sour cream

Mix together butter, shortening, and sugar until smooth. Add egg and vanilla. Sift together the dry ingredients. Then add to the batter alternating with the sour cream. Chill the dough for several hours, overnight is best.

Dust a rolling pin and work surface with extra flour. Then, in small batches, roll out the dough to ¼-inch thickness. Use your favorite cookie cutters to make shapes.

Place on parchment paper–covered cookie sheet. Bake at 375° for 10 to 12 minutes or until edges just begin to be golden brown.

Cool completely on wire rack. Now decorate with frosting and sprinkles. Enjoy!

The 12 Days of Christmas

And a partridge in a pear tree.

Frederic Austin

I loved the song, "The Twelve Days of Christmas" as a kid. It is so long and there is so much to remember. I felt very accomplished when I could belt out all the verses. And it was also fun to speed up as the list got longer just to prove to anyone listening that I really did know it very well. Turns out this song was, indeed, meant for children. "The Twelve Days of Christmas" was written some time in the 1700s to explain the faith to young Catholics.

Between 1558 and 1829, Catholics in England were not permitted to practice their faith openly. "The Twelve Days of Christmas" was one answer for keeping the faith alive and passing on the fundamentals. It was first published in 1780 as a chant, not a song. There was a secret meaning to each verse for those in the Church.

The "true love" mentioned in the song is not an earthly lover, but Jesus Christ Himself. He is the One giving all the good gifts. And He is represented as the partridge because those birds are known to protect their young by feigning injury to distract enemies.

This year, when you sing all the verses of this old carol, trying to remember if it's laying or leaping that comes next, you can know there are lessons hidden in the list. Here's what faithful Catholics were remembering as they sang this carol years ago:

A partridge in a pear tree: our Lord Jesus Christ

Two turtledoves: the Old and New Testaments

Three French hens: faith, hope, and charity

Four calling birds: the gospels: Matthew, Mark, Luke, and John

Five golden rings: the first five books of the Old Testament, which describe the Fall of man and the love of God in sending a Savior

Six geese a-laying: the six days of creation

Seven swans a-swimming: the gifts of the Holy Spirit: prophecy, serving, teaching, exhortation (encouragement, counsel), contribution, leadership, and mercy

Eight maids a-milking: the eight Beatitudes

Nine ladies dancing: the nine fruit of the Spirit

Ten lords a-leaping: the Ten Commandments

Eleven pipers piping: the eleven faithful apostles

Twelve drummers drumming: the twelve points of faith in the Apostles' Creed

Fill my mind with the tune of Your lessons.
Amen

Naming a Son

For a child is born to us, a son is given to us.
The government will rest on his shoulders. And he will be called:
Wonderful Counselor, Mighty God, Everlasting Father, Prince of Peace.
His government and its peace will never end.

Isaiah 9:6 NLT

saiah chapter 9, verse 6 is part of the powerful chorus in Handel's *Messiah*. It thunders out with great news of what we've been given, the gift of a Son. And I love that this verse lists a few of the names this Son will use. He will grow to be a Wonderful Counselor. He is our Mighty God. He is our Everlasting Father. He is the Prince of Peace.

Naming a child is serious business. When it came our turn to name an infant, we found out just how hard it could be. We started easy. We knew the last name. Done. Great, we were already a third of the way there!

In my husband's family, they pass down the name Rodney. Some men have it as their first name, others the middle. We wanted to honor the naming tradition of passing down a name. However, my husband never really liked the name Rodney. He goes by Rod. And what if we had a girl?

Rod's grandfather was named Lee Rodney. Lee is a name both a boy or a girl can wear with ease. So we decided to use that for our baby's middle name. Terrific, we were two-thirds of the way there. Now all we had to do was decide on a first name. What should it be? We chose Rachel for a girl. Somehow that was easy. But picking a boy's name eluded us. We tried looking in a baby-naming book and things just got silly fast as we tried out names like: Tiger, Hammer, Yogi, and Hermon.

Let's get serious—we have to pick something. The day I went into labor we packed our list of twelve boys' names in the overnight bag along with my toothbrush and clothes. Then, like hundreds of parents before us, we just seemed to know when our son was born that his name would be Zachary.

But the first years of his life we hardly called him Zachary. He had all kinds of nicknames. I am going to be kind and not share them all with you. Just know they are as silly as anything you've ever called your dear little ones. In fact, some of them are still in use.

This brings me back to the naming of our Savior. All the names put forth in the Bible are majestic and awe-inspiring. God really had a great list of names to choose from. But the name I think He uses with the most pleasure is Son. God gave us the *gift* of His Son.

Wonderful Counselor, Mighty God, Everlasting Father, Prince of Peace,
I am honored to call You my King. Thank You.
Amen

For unto us a Child is born
Unto us a Son is given

Home Sweet Home

I'll be home for Christmas, you can count on me,
if only in my dreams.

Kim Gannon

The melancholy tune "I'll Be Home for Christmas" was written in 1943. The lyrics are told from the point of view of a World War II soldier yearning to be home for the holidays. All the wishes for a lovely visit are there: snow, mistletoe, and presents under the tree. When Kim Gannon first pitched this song to those in the music industry, everyone passed, saying it was too sad. No one would want to be reminded of missing loved ones. Gannon kept trying, though. One day he was playing golf with Bing Crosby and pitched him the song. Bing decided to record it. "I'll Be Home for Christmas" became a seasonal standard.

Funny thing, naming a hurt helps you to get through it. The music industry wanted to gloss over the hurts of Christmas in 1943. They wanted to give everyone happy, upbeat tunes. But considering how popular this song became, the public knew a good thing when they heard it. Acknowledging pain lets you grieve over it.

Home is where most of us want to be for the holidays. Surrounded by those who know us best. The ones we want to hug and give gifts to. Separations come in all varieties. Geography, war, money, sickness—they can all keep us from where we long to be. Christmas is a hard time of year for many people. And all the festivities can make it worse.

You may be the one missing home this year. It feels like a very public hurt when you are left on the outside of holiday merrymaking. I don't have the magic words to ease that longing. Everyone suggests the usual fixes—distracting yourself, doing for others, waiting it out—but I suspect none of that helps. Naming your hurt gives you a place to start, a place to cry out to God. *Hey! I want to be with family! I am lonely! I am sad.* There is no magic wand to make it better and God may feel silent, but He does hear you. And He will listen as long as you want to cry.

My Christmas wish for you is to name the feelings you have this holiday (good, bad, or indifferent) and offer God the prayer of your heart. He is with you in your joy and in your pain.

I am missing the ones I love.
Ease my hurt and help me find a hint of Your love.
Amen

Check, Please!

Blessed is the season which engages the whole world in a conspiracy of love.
Hamilton Wright Mabie

Christmas is the time of year when we try to think differently about each other. We try kindness first. My friend Jeff told me about a Christmas season when he and his family tried a little extra kindness.

All four of his college kids were home for the Christmas holidays. The family went out to the movies, and on the way home they stopped at one of their favorite pizza joints. It was a Monday night. But for some reason the place was slammed. Jeff and his family were all talking and catching up. But no food arrived, so as the waitress sped by Jeff grabbed her arm and asked if their salads were up yet. She promised to bring them out as soon as she could. A few minutes later, Jeff apologized as she set down the salads.

"I am not upset. I just thought maybe the order got missed. We can see you're working hard. We're going to be your easiest table. Don't worry about us."

All the kids in the family had worked service jobs of one kind or another. Dealing with the public, especially the hungry masses, is stressful and underappreciated. Everyone at the table knew how difficult the evening was for their waitress. Other customers were even leaving in a huff. The family waited for an hour to get their food. When the bill came, Jeff suggested, "Let's leave her a big tip. What should it be?"

Without skipping a beat, his oldest daughter said a hundred dollars. *More than twice the bill!* Jeff thought maybe he'd round up to hundred. But the kids were having none of it. "Okay, we can leave a hundred-dollar tip, but it's going to cost us. We won't be able to go out to the movies next week. And there will be no lunch out after church." Everyone agreed. They were all in.

As they pulled out of the parking lot, Jeff looked back and could see the waitress huddled in conversation with the owner and another waitress. He smiled, knowing what they were talking about.

The next day Jeff ran into the restaurant owner. She told him she'd heard about the tip his family had left. "What you didn't know is that waitress is a single mom working her second job. She had just told her kids that day, there was not going to be enough money for Christmas gifts." Oh, wow.

The following Sunday Jeff and his family did not head out for brunch after church. They went straight home and made soup and sandwiches instead. The small change in their routine made a very merry difference in another household.

Give me the courage to act on my impulse to be generous and kind.
Make me bold even when it costs me to follow through.

Amen

Come & Worship

Angels from the realms of glory, wing your flight o'er all the earth.
Ye, who sang creation's story, now proclaim Messiah's birth.
Come and worship, come and worship, worship Christ the newborn King.

James Montgomery

I sing the alto part in our church choir. Altos parts are not fancy. We often land on one note and sit there for quite some time. If we have something jazzy to sing, you can be sure it's tricky and we have to practice a lot to get it right. Most often the sopranos are soaring around with the melody and we altos are chugging along with the counterbalance and harmonies.

I have a pleasing voice, but it's not a showcase solo voice. I am no good at sight-reading choral music. I can read music because I played the flute for years. I can see where the alto part is going—I just can't always hit the right pitches along the way. With a flute you press the right keys and blow; it's mechanical. With my voice sometimes I just hope I'm close, since I don't have keys to trust.

When I think of the heavenly choir announcing Jesus' birth, I kind of wonder about the altos. Was this a time they got a really impressive part? Was there more than one note for them to sing? Did they finally have a melody for the second verse?

Of course, I am looking at it all wrong. The altos didn't care what their part was; they were announcing the birth of Christ! They were thrilled to be part of the heavenly choir. They were in tune and out of their minds with joy.

I am not always so happy to be a supporting cast member. I feel small when my essential part is a foundation for the melody. I want someone to hear me. Is that true for you sometimes, too? You want a little recognition? Here's something you and I need to remember: Those altos added the countermelody that made the whole world sit up and take notice. Everyone listens for the heavenly choir.

Doing our part makes the whole a lot richer and more wonderful than any solo could ever be. The big booming announcement that it's time to come and worship the newborn King was delivered by all of heaven. Now it is our job to keep the chorus going. Every part is essential. It's up to each of us to share the story, whether we do so with the melody of the soprano line or the simple tones of the alto line. Come and worship! It's the best news we can sing.

I'm so excited about Your birth, Lord.
I will sing Your praises in my unique way with joy.
Amen

Surprise!

And he took bread, gave thanks and broke it, and gave it to them, saying,
"This is my body, given for you; do this in remembrance of me."
Luke 22:19

It's cinnamon bread!" The whisper spread down our pew at Christmas Eve services. Our whole extended family was sitting together. We were giggling and checking in with one another. We'd just taken communion and every one of us was licking our lips and enjoying the taste of cinnamon bread. Sugary, buttery, full of cinnamon yumminess. That can't be right? I was wondering if I could circle back and go through the communion line again just to make sure.

Communion was cinnamon bread? Who thought that was okay? Well, whoever it was—the ladies of church, the pastor, the choir director—someone had decided this Christmas Eve that we were really going to celebrate! What an unusual surprise. It gave me such joy.

I'll confess, communion doesn't always make me stop and pay attention. I miss the joy completely. There are times when I am at a retreat or a conference and special attention is paid to the celebration of the Eucharist. Then I do feel the holiness of the moment. Other times I don't let the sacredness of the act really sink in.

On Christmas Eve I am usually waiting to get to the yummy dinner or open a few presents or tuck into a warm bed after midnight services. I am waiting for the next thing. I am not thinking of the Lord's Table. So the year we had an unexpected treat at the communion table lives in my memory. It was a year I paused and truly remembered the beginning of the story: the birth of the Savior, which led to the saving of the world. We escaped death. That is cause for a joyous celebration.

Sometimes I still take communion for granted. It is more of a routine then a sacred moment. It is then, I try to remember the treasure of the time I was surprised by cinnamon bread at the communion table. The fact is, I should probably be surprised every time I approach the Lord's Table, because the King died for me.

Put peace in my heart so I can truly receive You the next time
I approach Your communion table, Lord.
Amen

Let Your Voice Ring

Go tell it on the mountain,
Over the hills and everywhere.
Go tell it on the mountain
That Jesus Christ is born!
John Wesley Work Jr.

When I was growing up, we used to put a stack of Christmas records on the turntable. We listened to holiday music all December long. We had a lot of classic albums by Andy Williams, Bing Crosby, Perry Como, Nat King Cole, and Jim Nabors, to name a few. I knew the records by heart. I loved singing along.

One song, though, gave me the giggles: Jim Nabors singing "Go, Tell It on the Mountain." At the time Jim Nabors played Gomer Pyle on a television sitcom. He talked in a goofy Southern accent. But on that record, when he sang, it was like thunder: a big, full voice. He literally announced the birth of Christ with his rendition of the song. As a child, I could not get past the fact that he sounded so different. It was hilarious to me.

Funny, yes, but the song and its message still ring in my head. The idea that we are to announce the birth of Christ from the mountaintops is exciting. If I am brave enough to do it. Sometimes I shrink from opportunities to exclaim the wonderful fact that Christ came to save the world. The Christmas season makes it easier for me to share my excitement and my faith. Even with the commercial side of the holiday irritating me with all kinds of messages to buy and give gifts, there are lots of reminders of the baby in the manger too. So it's natural to share the good news of Christ's birth and remind others that He is not a holiday decoration—He is our Savior.

What a spectacle to yell from the mountaintops for all of creation to hear! That is just how God did it, though. We read of a heavenly host announcing His birth (Luke 2:12–14). The story was so fantastic it was shared and shared until you and I know it today, thousands of years later. And we get to continue sharing the story.

Christ's birth is an astonishing truth. Makes you want to go out and tell everyone everywhere. And that is the point, right? We are so excited that Jesus Christ was born that we want to . . . *Go, tell it on the mountain, over the hills and everywhere!*

This Christmas, if you have the opportunity to share your faith story with someone, don't shrink from it. Let your voice ring with your faith and your love.

I pray for the gift of sharing our story, Lord: Your birth and my faith.
Amen

Traditions

Mele Kalikimaka is the thing to say,
On a bright Hawaiian Christmas Day.

Robert Alexander Anderson

Christmas is celebrated the world over. Every country has special things they do during this season and different greetings they offer to one another.

In Norway and Sweden, they wish each other "*God Jul.*" Many families still follow the tradition of keeping a large bowl of rice porridge outside for "*Nisse*" (or "elf"), who is known to play pranks on the animals in the barn. This is usually done on Christmas Eve in order to please him.

In the United States we say "*Merry Christma*s." A custom here is to decorate the outside of your house with lights. Many neighborhoods have a house or two that go all-out. Some communities even hold contests to see whose display is the most spectacular.

In Mexico the greeting is "*Feliz Navidad.*" The last two weeks of December everyone takes time off for parties and for visiting family. A tradition there is for youth to reenact Joseph and Mary's search for lodging with a procession. As the march continues, more people are added, playing angels, shepherds, and wise men. They sing traditional songs, and at the end there is a party for all.

The French say, "*Joyeux Noel*" to one another. In France the Christmas tree of America never became popular, instead they used a Yule log as a decoration of the season. This tradition is fading, but the traditional Yule log–shaped cake, *Buch de Nol,* is still going strong and is a very yummy part of the French holiday.

And "*Mele Kalikimaka*" is the Hawaiian Christmas greeting. The holiday came to the Hawaiian Islands from missionaries in the eighteenth century. Previously there was a festival called Makahiki, which lasted around four months and in which all wars were forbidden. (Brilliant!) Today people still celebrate with big meals and parties, but Christmas songs are played on guitars and ukuleles and they go to the beach.

Wherever you live you have a unique way of celebrating the season, too: special songs, yummy treats, nostalgic music, lovely stories, and unique decorations. Some things come from your heritage, and others may have been adopted over time. At my house we put origami-folded balls over each light on our Christmas tree. It started when we saw it a magazine years ago and now it's one of our favorite decorations.

Hopefully some of your traditions help you center the season on the true meaning of the whole celebration. For me, lighting the Advent wreath at the dinner table each evening helped me focus on Jesus' coming, not Santa. It was one of the few times of the year we ate by candlelight. I couldn't miss the glow of love around the table.

What tradition helps you remember Jesus in this season?

Thank You for all the lovely ways to greet the holiday
and celebrate with traditions that warm our hearts.

Amen

HOW TO FOLD A CHRISTMAS BALL

PUT A PAPER BALL OVER EVERY LIGHT ON YOUR TREE!

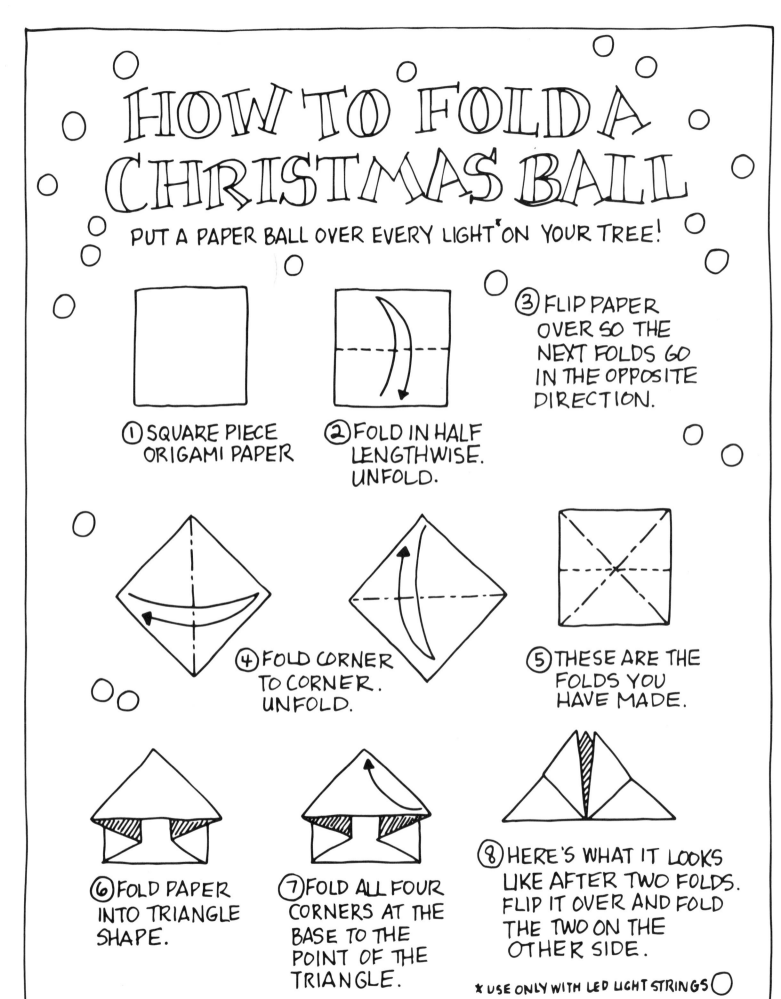

① SQUARE PIECE ORIGAMI PAPER

② FOLD IN HALF LENGTHWISE. UNFOLD.

③ FLIP PAPER OVER SO THE NEXT FOLDS GO IN THE OPPOSITE DIRECTION.

④ FOLD CORNER TO CORNER. UNFOLD.

⑤ THESE ARE THE FOLDS YOU HAVE MADE.

⑥ FOLD PAPER INTO TRIANGLE SHAPE.

⑦ FOLD ALL FOUR CORNERS AT THE BASE TO THE POINT OF THE TRIANGLE.

⑧ HERE'S WHAT IT LOOKS LIKE AFTER TWO FOLDS. FLIP IT OVER AND FOLD THE TWO ON THE OTHER SIDE.

✱ USE ONLY WITH LED LIGHT STRINGS

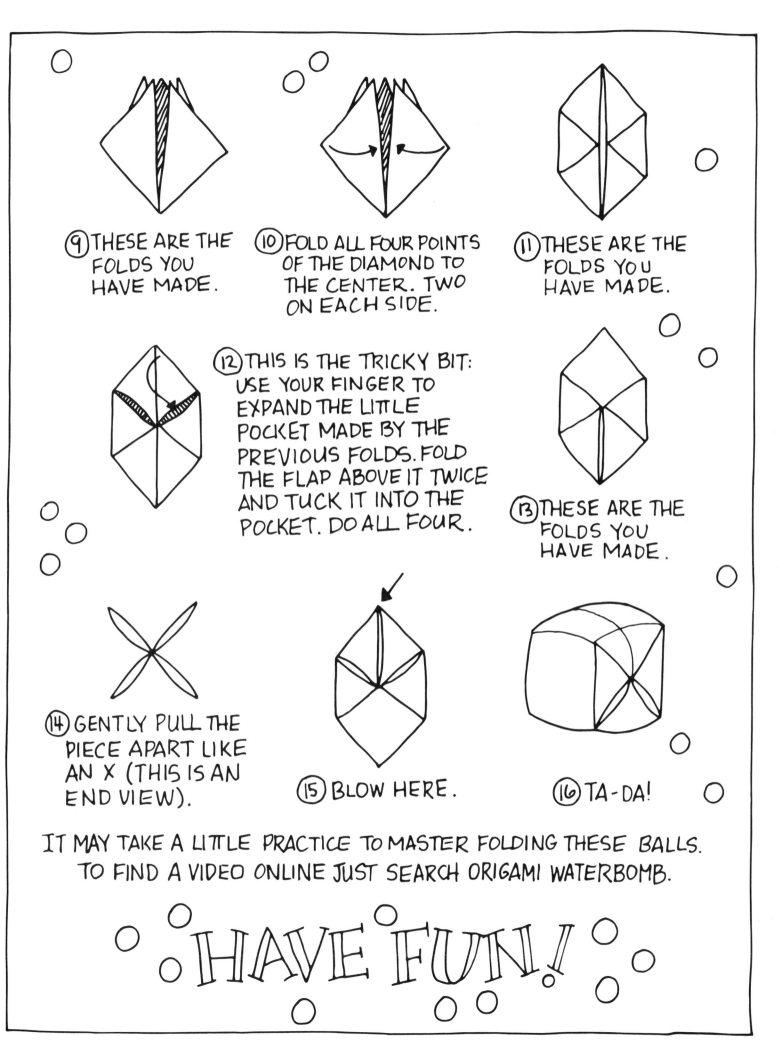

⑨ THESE ARE THE FOLDS YOU HAVE MADE.

⑩ FOLD ALL FOUR POINTS OF THE DIAMOND TO THE CENTER. TWO ON EACH SIDE.

⑪ THESE ARE THE FOLDS YOU HAVE MADE.

⑫ THIS IS THE TRICKY BIT: USE YOUR FINGER TO EXPAND THE LITTLE POCKET MADE BY THE PREVIOUS FOLDS. FOLD THE FLAP ABOVE IT TWICE AND TUCK IT INTO THE POCKET. DO ALL FOUR.

⑬ THESE ARE THE FOLDS YOU HAVE MADE.

⑭ GENTLY PULL THE PIECE APART LIKE AN X (THIS IS AN END VIEW).

⑮ BLOW HERE.

⑯ TA-DA!

IT MAY TAKE A LITTLE PRACTICE TO MASTER FOLDING THESE BALLS. TO FIND A VIDEO ONLINE JUST SEARCH ORIGAMI WATERBOMB.

HAVE FUN!

The Center of the Season

O come, O come, Emmanuel,
Rejoice! Rejoice! Emmanuel
Shall come to thee, O Israel.

Unknown

Do you worry that Christ is slipping out of your Christmas celebration? I do when I look at my to-do lists that seem to stretch into next year. Yikes! If only I scaled back. If only I took a break. If only I reached out and asked God for help.

In the gospel of Mark (5:24–34) there is a story of a desperate woman reaching out. She had suffered from bleeding for twelve years. She had heard Jesus was healing people. *If only . . .* she thought. *If only I touch the hem of His robe, I will be healed.* She believed the tiniest contact would make everything all right. And she dared to do it. In the midst of a crowd she got close enough to reach out. Immediately she was healed. And in that moment, Jesus knew it too. He searched her out in the crowd and said, "Daughter, your faith has healed you. Go in peace and be freed from your suffering."

Of course my "problem" of distraction during the holidays is not nearly as serious as a chronic illness that resulted in woman being shunned in society. But when my distraction is running my life, God is still ready, willing, and more than able to heal me from that affliction. He can change my focus with the tiniest contact. He can put Himself in the center of my Christmas season and my whole New Year if I will only ask. And it is my prayer to ask: *Come, Emmanuel. I want to rejoice and celebrate Your life-changing arrival into the world.*

God can put Himself in the center of your thinking and feelings during this happy time of year. Ask. Reach out and take the tiniest step in prayer toward Him. He will fill your mind with the true meaning of the season, His birth, the beginning of His story on earth that ends with your redemption.

Jesus, take the tiny opening I am giving and find a huge place in my heart.
Let me live in this holiday season with joy, not distraction.
Amen

The Gift of Love

For God so loved the world that he gave his one and only Son,
that whoever believes in him shall not perish but have eternal life.

John 3:16

Many people know this famous reference even if they have never picked up a Bible. They may not know any other verse address, but they have heard of John 3:16. It describes a sacrifice of true love. It's the ultimate gift. I've seen it written on building walls, under freeways, on plaques, and in church newsletters. I've even seen it on a poster in the stands of NFL football games on national television. This verse can pop up anywhere and everywhere.

God loves us, and we have no idea how much. Seriously. There are no words I can magically write in a short devotion that will convey the enormity of that statement. Even as I am writing this, it's hard to grasp the gravity of what I just boldly put on paper: *God gave His Son so we can have eternal life.* It's a mystery and a glorious gift.

The pools of God's love are without end. Just when I think God has poured out as much love as I'll ever need, or am entitled to, I find more. His supply is unending. There is enough for everyone, every single person on the face of the earth. Every person ever born and every person to come. All of us. No limit.

Christmas is a season of love. It's the season of John 3:16. We are celebrating God coming to earth to start His love fest with the human race *in person.* This is one of the great mysteries of our faith: God becoming human. *And to believe this fact is to want to celebrate it.*

"Thank You" is such a small expression of my gratitude for your sacrifice. But it is what I have, a humble heart. I will try to honor You with a Christmas season centered on You and Your gift to me.

Dear Lord, with a grateful heart
I say thank You for the gift of Your Son, Jesus.
Amen

Small Wonders

But you, O Bethlehem Ephrathah, are only a small village
among all the people of Judah. Yet a ruler of Israel,
whose origins are in the distant past, will come from you on my behalf.
Micah 5:2 NLT

I am small of stature, five-foot-three. I don't always like being small. I take to heart some of the synonyms for small including: *inconsequential, inadequate,* and *insufficient.* That is how I feel sometimes: *insufficient,* lacking for the job at hand.

If Bethlehem had feelings, it would probably think it was inadequate too. Poor little town, not even enough hotel rooms for crowds of visitors. Bethlehem was not really adequate for a royal birth. But we all know the name of this little village. Bethlehem, you are the birthplace of our Savior.

Small matters. With one small breath, God made man. With one little word, Mary became the mother of God. With one modest invitation, an innkeeper found a room for a King. And with one tiny word of love, we can give another joy. Doing our humble parts is important.

Bethlehem had no clue how significant it would one day be. It was a sleepy little place that became the birthplace of Jesus. We, too, have no idea how consequential our actions will be. Our small gifts of loving-kindness to each other can reap big benefits. One of those outcomes may be as simple as a peaceful Christmas season, a year when you know more joy by doing small things.

Sending a special Christmas card with a handwritten message to an old friend. Taking an extra plate of cookies to the office or sharing them with a neighbor. Driving with courtesy and safety in busy holiday traffic. Finding small ways to be kind and bring peace show your big heart for the world. And who knows how long these acts will last? Bethlehem never thought it would be more than a pinpoint on a map and yet we sing of the everlasting light shining in its streets long ago:

O little town of Bethlehem, how still we see thee lie.
Above thy deep and dreamless sleep the silent stars go by.
Yet in thy dark streets shineth the everlasting light.
The hopes and fears of all the years are met in thee tonight.
Philip Brooks

May my small gifts of love bring big moments of peace and joy.
Amen

Take a Break

In the meadow we can build a snowman,
Walkin' in a winter wonderland.
Richard B. Smith

Winter means snow. At least that is what I thought until we lived in California for twenty years. Winter there means a mix of sunshine and rain. It's odd weather for Christmas if you ask this Midwest girl. I distinctly remember snowdrifts as tall as the house when I grew up in Chicago, or icicles nearly touching the ground on my grandma's house in Wisconsin. Winter might have been harsh, but it was Christmas-card picturesque. (And as a kid, I never had to worry about driving in it.)

When I first moved to California, sunny, warm December days made it hard for me to get in the holiday spirit. *This isn't winter. This is constant spring.* I know what you are thinking, why would I complain? No shoveling. No icy roads. No frozen pipes. No slippery sidewalks. No problems. True enough. But there was also no reason to wear cozy winter sweaters or drink hot chocolate. No snowmen or snow angels. No sledding. No fires in the hearth.

I finally came to appreciate the California winter. There was never a reason to stay indoors. It was lovely to take a break from the holiday rush and go for a hike. I might have missed the first snowfall of the season, but I got to go to the beach.

Now we again live where there are proper winters and my heart thrills at the sight of snow. Lovely as California is, I prefer my Christmases to be white. Maybe you live in a place where you are knee-deep in holiday atmosphere. It's hard to get around, even dangerous sometimes. But the quiet after a snowfall is a lovely time to go *"walkin' in a winter wonderland."*

It is my hope for your holiday season that you can get out and enjoy whatever kind of winter there is where you live. Sunny or snowy, taking a walk outside will really clear your head at this busy time of year. Take a break and enjoy some winter.

Your world, Lord, is a winter wonderland whether it's green or white.
Thank You for fresh air and beautiful seasons.
Amen

"FOR I KNOW THE PLANS I HAVE FOR YOU,"
DECLARES THE LORD
"PLANS TO PROSPER YOU & GIVE YOU"

Rise Up & Follow

There's a star in the east on Christmas morn,
Rise up, shepherd, and follow.
It will lead to the place where the Savior's born,
Rise up, shepherd, and follow.

African American Spiritual

Sometimes, in the weeks leading up to Christmas, we have our heads down. We concentrate on all the things we want to accomplish to make this a perfect holiday. We bake cookies. We address cards. We shop for presents. We wrap gifts. We clean house. We throw parties. We go caroling. We arrange travel plans. We go a little overboard.

I like all the trappings of the holiday season. I used to get carried away with lovely ideas of how to enhance the celebration. I have pared down some over the years. Yet I still have a hefty to-do list of things I feel might just be essential for me and my family's holiday enjoyment. We must have sugar cookies, after all.

The simple song "Rise Up, Shepherd, and Follow" is an invitation to stop the holiday frenzy. The song asks the shepherds to leave their sheep (lambs, ewes, rams, and the whole flock). Follow the star. Come to Bethlehem. See the Savior. That star is calling us just as it was the shepherds all those years ago. Instead of leaving our sheep, we are called to leave the cooking, the shopping, the wrapping, and the decorating.

Rise up, see what's next. All the tinsel will be packed away in a couple of weeks. Christmas will be over and we will be different, or just tired and broke from doing and spending instead of seeing and following. Holiday preparations are great and it's fun to indulge, as long as we remember why we are doing it. Use your time of preparation to take a step toward God. Don't miss the point. The point is following the star for the rest of the year.

When this Christmas is over and we put away all the decorations, we are still called to follow. Follow our Savior into the New Year and new lives. All our preparations are not lost. Christ gives us a reason to celebrate, not His birth, but His life and sacrifice. Continue the excitement. We found a Savior in the manger to follow Him in life, not just through a holiday.

Christmas sparkles and when all the decorations are
put away in a box, I still want to follow You, Lord.
Help me continue the celebration of Your birth throughout the year.
Amen

Silly Songs

Jingle bell, jingle bell, jingle bell rock,
Jingle bells swing and jingle bells ring.
Joseph Carleton Beal & James Ross Boothe

This is a holy season of the year celebrating the birth of our Lord. This is also the season of parties. From office to church and home again, there is eggnog flowing and cookies for the taking. There is Chex Mix and candlelight. We decorate with mangers and snowmen. The holy and the hilarious live side by side this time of year. Throwing a holiday party is a Christmas tradition. There are special treats we make just once a year: cookies, cakes, bars, nuts, candy, dips, big feasts of every variety. This is the time of year when we indulge.

Music is a big part of Christmas. There are lots of sacred songs to celebrate the season, and they eloquently tell about the Nativity story. There are those silly songs that are favorites we pull out each year: "I Saw Mommy Kissing Santa Claus," "All I Want for Christmas Is My Two Front Teeth," and of course, "Grandma Got Run over by a Reindeer." These are part of Christmas, too, and just as nostalgic as "O Holy Night" and "O Come, All Ye Faithful." We hear it all on the radio and in shopping malls.

Enjoying the serious and the silly is part of what makes Christmas a whole and human event. This is a birthday party after all. We are thrilled the Savior is born, but we also want a pound of peppermint bark and a round of "Jingle Bell Rock." We make merry and we feel blessed at the same time.

Wanting to hear Bing Crosby sing about a white Christmas or listen to chipmunks singing about Hula-Hoops has become a fun and expected part of our celebrations. It's when the balance gets tipped toward the ridiculous that we realize we've gone too far. When there is more sugar and silliness than silence and sacredness, that's when you know your celebration is missing something.

Christmas is supposed to be fun. It comes only once a year, but remember to celebrate the heavenly gift of the season, too. Happily, that comes every day of the year.

Silly songs of Christmas make my heart sing just as much as the sacred ones.
Thank You for the complete celebration of Your birth.
Amen

AWAY IN A MANGER

HOLY NIGHT

roasting on an open fire

I WONDER AS I WANDER

3 I SAW SHIPS

faithful

Clearing the Way

Joshua told the people,
"Consecrate yourselves, for tomorrow the LORD
will do amazing things among you."
Joshua 3:5

I have the luxury of a cleaning crew coming to my house twice a month. Every other Tuesday I spend the morning getting ready. I do laundry so the sheets are fresh. I declutter. I put away all the things I have pulled out on my desk, and the end tables and countertops. I clear out for them because it makes their job easier and more efficient.

As I was picking up today, it occurred to me that I am getting ready for another arrival as well. In this Christmas season, I am preparing for the Savior to come. And for that reason I should clean my spiritual house too. What does it take to get my spirit ready? I can declutter my mind. I can push aside all the extras of Christmas and focus on just my Savior. Right, like that is easy. The commercial part of Christmas is screaming at me from all angles. Nonetheless I try.

The cleaners come on a regular basis, and that means my house never becomes a complete disaster. Cleaning my soul happens on a regular basis too. Going to church on Sunday helps; weekly choir practice and quiet time helps. Those things are all ways for me to refocus and declutter.

Christmas is a time when I would like to go deeper. I want to be ready for God to come. So, as I can in my morning quiet time, I think of this season with renewed awe. I wait for God to meet me and to clean me further. I want to be ready for the work He has in mind for me to do in the New Year. Sometimes I suspect the work I am supposed to do is more cleaning of my spirit. But whatever He has for me, I want to be open and ready.

You can prepare too. Think of what cleaning you'd like to do. Maybe just knowing God will come and help you with whatever cleaning project you need is enough to get you started.

Getting ready for my cleaners takes me a morning. Getting ready for Christ takes me a lifetime. I do my best to prepare and anticipate being used in His service. None of us will ever be as bright and shiny as we could be, but the grace-filled truth is that God will use us anyway in amazing ways.

I am cleaning house for You, Lord. Come and use me.
Amen

Imagine

Angels we have heard on high
Sweetly singing o'er the plains.
And the mountains in reply
Echoing their joyous strains.
Gloria in excelsis deo.

French Carol

I love the image at the beginning of this carol: sweet singing and mountains echoing. Can you picture it? It's a calm night. Stars are beginning to twinkle overhead. The shepherds are talking softly as they bed down the sheep. Every creature is settling in for the night.

And then a tune comes over the hills, echoing all around, filling the air with a chorus. Is this a threat? But it sounds wonderful. A feeling of joy must have filled them. Angels appear! The shepherds stare in confusion. Though they were astonished, I am sure they soon realized this was not something they needed to fight. This was an otherworldly experience. This was heaven opening to sing to them directly.

The first thing angels always say when they appear in Bible stories is, "Don't be afraid." But who could *not* be afraid? It's an angel! I would be thunderstruck. I'm sure the shepherds were scared. But the Christmas angel gave them very good news. I think they felt joy in their hearts before they heard the news with their ears. The glow of love filled them. What a concert: a moonlit night, a purple sky, black mountains, and a heavenly chorus singing of God's love.

This was such monumental news that they left their flocks. Leaving your flock was a huge offense, criminal in fact. Yet they were drawn to the manger by heavenly direction. God is on earth NOW. Come and see. Come adore on bended knee. The whole night is one that would live with the shepherds for the rest of their lives. The whole amazing night lives for us too, through the Scriptures.

Imagining scenes like shepherds meeting angels help me focus the Christmas season on more holy ground. I take a little time to really think about this season of love. I think of those shepherds long ago, those frightened boys. Glory visited them in the middle of the night and filled their hearts with wonder. They were scared yet exhilarated.

When I slow down enough in all my holiday prep to imagine a heavenly choir filling the night, it opens up thoughts of wonder. I can get almost as thunderstruck as those shepherds. An angel whispers in my ear too: God is on earth NOW. You do not need to rush out and take action; you need to remember this divine thought and take joy.

Glorious! May strains of joy fill my thoughts today.
God came to earth!
Amen

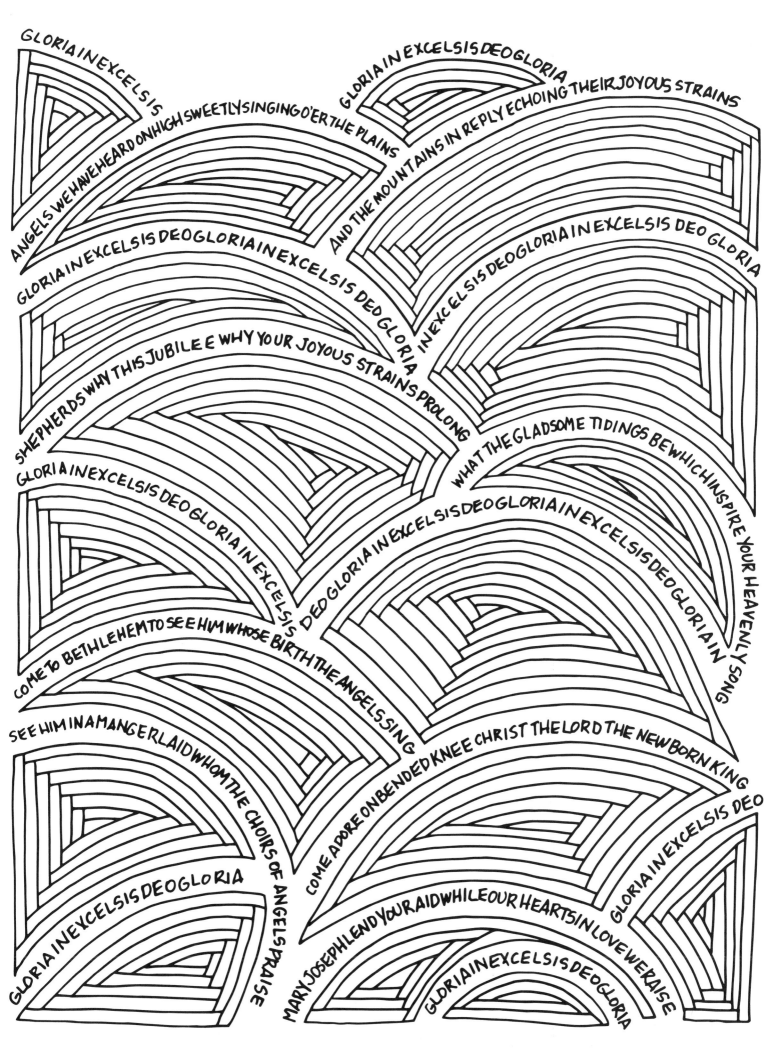

The Gift of Your Heart

Love is enough . . .
When there's nothing left to give the Lord, then you have to look at what you have.
Your soul. Yourself. And that is the only gift He wants from His children.

Bodie Thoene

Have you ever made a gift for your parents at Christmastime? I was a Girl Scout for years. I have made my share of tie racks, pot holders, and stationery sets. I've given my parents gifts from the heart, if not from the store. My mom and dad loved me and the gift was incidental. As a child I wanted to have something tangible to show them I loved them. The smiles and joy from those offerings are more vivid in my memory than the times when I could afford the perfect sweater or appliance or new gadget to give my parents.

Maybe you are searching for the perfect gift for that special someone? Trying to find the one thing that will tell this person exactly how you feel? You want to give the thing that will bring a smile and let the other person know *"I love you so very much."* It's hard to wrap up that much love in the ideal gift.

God is not looking for the perfect gift from you. There is only one thing He wants. In fact, you do not even have to brave the mall to find His heart's desire. He is waiting for you to offer your soul. He is waiting for you to come willingly. To bring Him the one thing only you can give. You already have the perfect gift, because *you* are the perfect gift.

In whatever shape you are right now, this very moment, frazzled or bedazzled, you are the one thing God wants most this Christmas. He longs to take you into His care. God knows there is treasure in your heart. He also knows just what He can do with the gift only you can give. He wants to use His new gift to show more people in the world His heart so the cycle of love will continue.

Remember to put love on your gift-giving list. This season, in all the bustle of trying to find the right gifts to share with your loved ones, remember to wrap your heart in the shiniest paper you can find and offer it again to the King who came to earth. Your heart is the only thing He has ever wanted from you.

I am giving You the gift of my heart, Lord.
Amen

Christmas Lullaby

Silent night, holy night,
All is calm, all is bright.
Josef Mohr

During the Christmas season of 1818, Assistant Pastor Josef Mohr of St. Nicholas' Church in Oberndorf, Austria, saw a local performance of the nativity story. On his way home from the presentation, he was musing over the story and remembered a poem he had penned some years earlier. His poem, he thought, would make a lovely carol for his congregation. Only trouble was, he had no tune and the organ at the church was broken. Still, he took his idea to the church organist, Franz Gruber, and asked if he could set the poem to music. Mohr made his request on Christmas Eve. With only a few hours to work, Gruber rose to the task and composed a lovely guitar tune for the evening service. *"Stille Nacht"* was sung for the first time that night and quickly became a favorite.

That is all history. Yet "Silent Night" still beats strong. The song is often sung like a meditative lullaby, sweet and light. Singing to and about the Christ child got me thinking.

Jesus came to earth as a baby, a real human baby, one who needed comfort. The tune we sing about Him presents the picture of a baby so calm and heavenly. But I wonder. Human babies only know their human needs. Jesus had not yet grown to maturity. He cried when He was hungry. He got cold and fussed to be cuddled and warmed. He needed clothing and food and love from Mary and Joseph. He was real.

When I think of Jesus as a baby on earth, so many images come to mind. Though the tune was written nearly two thousand years after His birth, I can picture Mary leaning in closely to her new infant son and soothing Him with the "Silent Night" lullaby. There must have been some tune or words she hummed into His ear to settle His heart. I picture Mary cooing to Jesus, "Hush, little baby, hear Your mama's voice. You are safe in my arms."

"Silent Night" is the perfect tune to hum in this season when we are celebrating the birth of Jesus. He was a baby first, unbelievable as that is to understand. Jesus wanted the touch of His mama in the manger. He needed the strength of His papa when Herod later hunted Him. Jesus was a helpless child, loved and protected Himself before He was a grown preacher. It is sweet to think of our infant Savior and sing Him a lullaby.

You are our heavenly Father, but at Christmastime we celebrate Your infant birth.
Thank You again for sending sweet Jesus to earth.
Amen

Locked in My Heart

But Mary treasured up all these things and pondered them in her heart.

Luke 2:19

Mary has an amazing testimony, a faith story like no other. She was visited by an angel and told she would be the mother of God. Incredible as that was, her adventure was just beginning.

Through her pregnancy God assured Mary, kept Joseph at her side, and brought her safely to Bethlehem. Mary delivered a baby, the Son of God, just as it was foretold to her. Then, from shepherds to wise men, the world began to hear of her story. But the new family was in danger and fled to Egypt with God's protection. And that's where the story ends for a while.

The Bible doesn't tell us all the details of Jesus growing up. Just like every other child on earth, the drama of the birth gave way to everyday life. Mary had to change diapers, breastfeed, travel home again. She was a working mom, working hard at raising her son and running her home. She was Joseph's helpmate and a good wife.

There was probably not a lot of downtime for Mary to prayerfully think of her experience. She and Joseph were busy with the day-to-day details of raising their son. Still, like any mother, Mary must have looked at her son with joy and confusion. Joy: *He's perfect, I love Him so dearly.* Confusion: *Why does He do the things He does?*

Each event in her journey with Jesus gave her more to think about. She must have had so many questions. Pondering questions and treasuring events is a way of connecting with God, of praising Him even in uncertainty. I'm sure sometimes Mary wondered, *Did that really happen?* Other times she smiled with joy at the certain memory that *yes*, it did happen. She held the memories close, and I bet they comforted her as much as they astonished her.

Mary's story always makes me wonder. Would I have handled this situation as well as Mary did? Would I have had that kind of faith? I'm not sure I would have. Yet I do have a faith story. Mine is one of slow growth over a lifetime through times of doubt and times of conviction. All of it adds up to my belief in the Father in heaven who loves me.

Sometimes I wonder about the things that have happened to me. Why events turned out as they have. Pondering my own story in my heart is an exercise of praise. I am in awe that the God of the universe has His fingerprints all over my life. Maybe Mary pondered her life the same way. She gave birth to the Son of God. *O Lord, why me? I am so humbled by the honor.* Surely it would take her a lifetime to grasp.

Father, I hold my faith in my heart and marvel over it.
You gave it to me. Help me keep it strong.

Amen

Everyday Reminders

Oh, the fullness, pleasure, sheer excitement of knowing God on earth!
Elisabeth Elliot

God came to earth! That is the best news of the Christmas season. And the excitement continues, because God is still among us as the Holy Spirit. He shows up all the time. Be on the lookout.

I look for God showing up. I love to find Him at work. Because I keep an eye out, I see Him personally in large and small ways. He is everywhere in my life. If I awake from a deep sleep to find a writing idea in my mind, it feels like a whisper from God showing me a metaphor to strengthen my faith.

Or I sit in choir rehearsal struggling with a complicated part. Then with practice, it becomes clear and I can sing God's praise rather than worry about the right notes. I feel God's help give me patience to practice and sing well in the group.

Or when my annoyance with technology reaches a boiling point, that is just the moment when someone sends me a cheery email. I forget my frustrations and feel God's good care calming my day. He seemed to know I was in need of a smile.

Or when I enjoy a little holiday merriment by listening to a concert, or singing along with the radio, or reading a good story, I feel God's love in this happy season.

These are just a few examples of looking for God moving in my life. There are so many. You can find them in your life too. Good food. Holiday music. Christmas decorations. Meeting with friends. Cards in the mail. Call from a relative. Look and you will see and feel blessed by all the little ways God is showing you His loving care.

God is in the world every day, not just Christmas Day. He shows up all the time with good things here on earth. How exciting! What a joy!

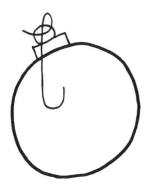

I'm excited, God, to know You are still here on earth,
showing me Your loving care through the Holy Spirit.
Thank You, Lord.
Amen

THE FULLNESS, PLEASURE, **SHEER** excitement OF **KNOWING** GOD ON earth

Joy to the World

Joy to the world, the Lord is come!
Let earth receive her King.
Let every heart prepare Him room,
And heaven and nature sing.

Isaac Watts

Joy to the world! The Lord has come! We are filled with joy! Use as many exclamation points as possible! Stop right there. This is not proper. We don't do things this way. And furthermore "Joy to the World" is not even a Christmas hymn.

That's right. One of the most popular Christmas carols was written as a celebration of the end of days. Isaac Watts penned "Joy to the World" in the early eighteenth century. He used Psalm 98 as his inspiration for the hymn. Using biblical text only for inspiration writing a song using your own words was not accepted in 1719.

Isaac Watts is now considered the "father of English Hymnody" with over six hundred hymns to his credit. But his music did not follow the conventions of his day. In the 1700s the only songs sung in church services were metrical psalms. Which means the literal words of scripture, no additions and certainly no omissions.

Watts had other ideas. He didn't reject metrical psalms; he simply wanted to see them more impassioned. *"They ought to be translated in such a manner as we have reason to believe David would have composed them if he had lived in our day,"* he wrote. He wanted the everyday man to understand and be moved by music in a church service.

His critics were not impressed, calling his work flights of fantasy since they left out too much of any psalm to be considered scripture anymore. Watts continued to write his music, and so today we have a rich collection, including "O God, Our Help in Ages Past" and "When I Survey the Wondrous Cross." He worked with passion even though many dismissed his music.

Watts stuck with his ideas. He offered his passion to God, and his music has remained beloved for centuries. *Joy to the world!* We sing it today and we understand the thrill of celebrating the Lord's coming to earth. We have the hymn because a composer followed his convictions and gave us his gift.

Heaven, and nature, and I will sing with joy for my King.
Amen

Refresh and Refocus

As the deer pants for streams of water,
so my soul pants for you, my God.
My soul thirsts for God, for the living God.
When can I go and meet with God?

Psalm 42:1–2

When my son was little, we were members at the Bay Area Discovery Museum in Sausalito, California. We went all the time. He spent hours playing on his favorite interactive exhibits. He climbed aboard the fishing boat and pretended to steer the vessel out to sea to catch crabs. He pulled on construction gear and pretended to build a high-rise apartment building. He crawled, dug, scooped, glued, sang, painted, and baked. It was (and still is) a great place for a toddler to spend the day.

We attended the opening of a new *Alice in Wonderland* exhibit. The place was packed. Everyone was having a good time. There was no pushing or shoving, just lots of excitement and smiles. The moms were having fun too. The interactive exhibit was very well designed. Kids pretended to have tea parties. They played with giant cards. They squealed with happiness.

I watched as my son climbed over a giant toadstool. Then I felt a little hug around my legs. I looked down and a toddler looked up at my face and burst into tears. In a sea of moms wearing blue jeans, this youngster had latched on to his mom for safety. Except when he looked up, he didn't see his mom's face. He'd hugged the wrong set of legs. He panicked. It was easy for me to find his mom and attach him to the right set of arms ready to hug him. *"That was an easy mistake to make with all these blue-jeans legs."* The other mom laughed too and settled her toddler.

This got me thinking: How many times do I attach myself to the wrong set of legs? How often do I look up and see I am far away from my Father in heaven? I too cry out with the realization that I am stuck in the wrong place. Christmas is a season when it is easy to drift to the wrong place. I get caught up with holiday busyness and forget to pause and think of the heavenly purpose.

Sometimes I need the reminder several times to focus on the meaning of the season. It's okay. God forgives my distraction. Each morning I can reach for His hand and we can walk together. I will probably tug away and get distracted again. But He'll be right there as a loving parent waiting for me to come back.

I want to hug You close, Father. Help me latch on to You this Christmas.

Amen

A Sign of the times

Beat the holiday rush. Come in this week.
Church Sign

There is a church in my neighborhood with a sign in front that they change every week. Sometimes they announce an upcoming event like a picnic or a concert, but most often they use their sign for levity and to make the community think in a positive way. I've seen them post things like:

WE SPECIALIZE IN SOUL FOOD.

THERE ARE SOME QUESTIONS THAT CAN'T BE ANSWERED BY GOOGLE.

A LOT OF KNEELING WILL KEEP YOU IN GOOD STANDING.

PRAYER: THE BEST WIRELESS CONNECTION.

The sign usually makes me smile and often makes me think. The first week of December it read: *Beat the holiday rush. Come in this week.* What a good thought. Lots of folks go to church just twice a year, Easter and Christmas. (In fact, one year the Monday morning after Easter, the sign in front of the church read: *We are here between Easter and Christmas too.*) This was a reminder to keep Christ in Christmas.

Here is a congregation taking note of the busy holiday season and gently suggesting we come now to celebrate. Their sign may be a tongue-in-cheek invitation, but it is an invitation nonetheless. They are asking the community to please remember to find time for the holy in their holiday. They are suggesting folks come share the Christmas season with them longer than just for the Christmas Eve services.

I like that this church does not seem to take itself too seriously. They seem to be saying: *We get it. We know you are busy. It's Christmas. But it's quiet in here. We have what you are searching for, and not just at Christmas but always.*

Perhaps I am reading way too much into a simple sign in front of a neighborhood church. But if it made me think, then it's doing the job intended. First a smile, then a pause to think that, yes, I want to find the sacred in this holiday season. This is not my home church, but they have become part of my holiday nonetheless, because as I drive by I am reminded to beat the holiday rush and keep the sacred in my heart every day.

Thank You for the reminders to keep the holy in our Christmas holiday.
Amen

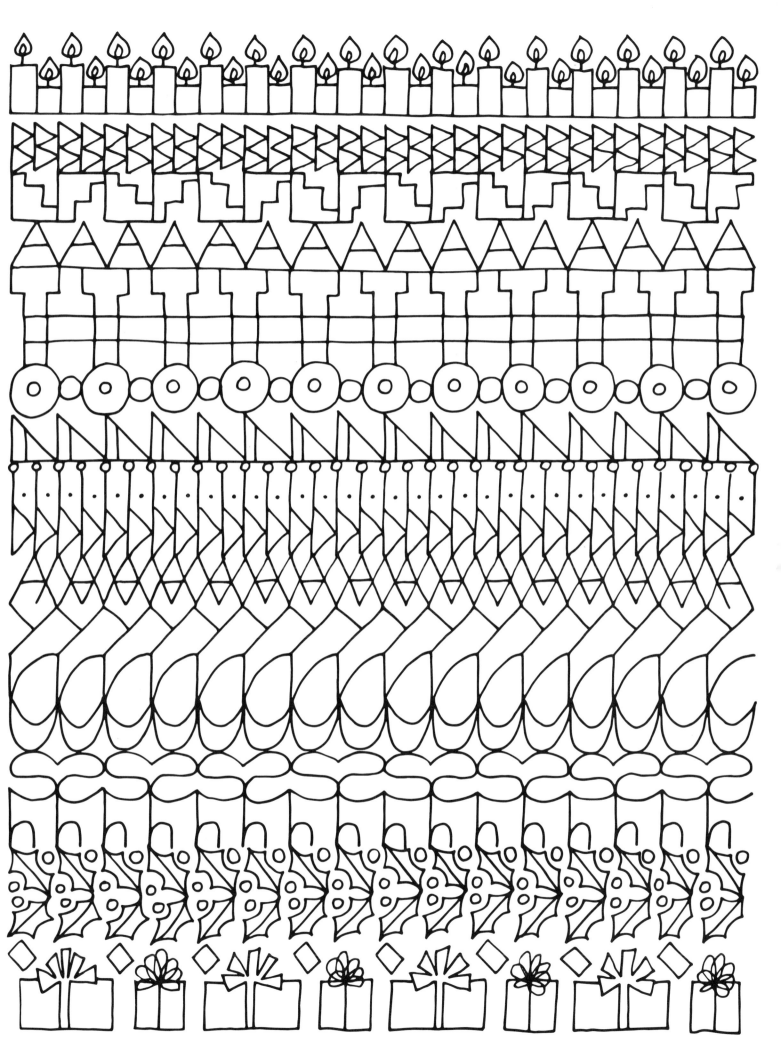

The Perfect Gift

Our finest gifts we bring, pa rum pum, pum, pum.

Katherine Kennicott Davis

I like Christmas shopping. I like browsing seasonal boutiques. I especially like finding something unexpected. I like it so much that some years I don't stop. I buy a few things in January at the after-Christmas sales. I tuck those things away for the following year. Yes, there is always a chance I'll forget where I hid them from curious family members, but I do it anyway.

I also like making Christmas gifts. Some can be whipped up in the season, like baked goodies and craft projects. And other gifts take months, like a hand-knit sweater or a lovely scrapbook. I like the planning and gathering of supplies. I like the hours spent creating. I really like thinking about my loved one while I'm working.

The little drummer boy in the famous song hadn't been shopping. He didn't have weeks to prepare. He was caught short. The wise men had just delivered very expensive gifts from countries far away. How could a little drummer boy compete?

It's an interesting exercise to wonder what you would bring the Christ child if you were asked at the last minute. It might be a lullaby sung in your beautiful voice. Or could it be the gift of a meal for His parents? Maybe you would offer to cuddle the infant so Mary could have a rest. And if you had a month to prepare, what would you do? Some speedy knitters might cast on a sweater or blanket. Or a wood carver might make a toy. What if you had a year?

Let me clue you in: You have a lifetime. God wants all your good gifts. The best you can offer in any form will make Him smile. A freshly mowed lawn for an elderly neighbor. A well-organized meeting run with efficiency for a busy staff. A balanced meal served to a hungry family. A safely traveled road delivering the carpool to work and school on time. The best garden, painting, balance sheet, photograph, app, cookies, dress, brick wall, washed car, kicked ball, swung golf club, sung song—all given to God with joy. God has a very long wish list of things He loves to get for Christmas, and the joy is that we can deliver our gifts all year long.

I offer my life as a gift to You, Lord.

Amen

Our finest gifts we bring

A Christmas Special

Hark, the herald angels sing,
Glory to the newborn King.
Charles Wesley

Hark, the Herald Angels Sing" is one of the first carols I ever learned to play on my flute. I loved being able to play it whenever the mood struck me . . . and, yes, sometimes the mood struck me in the middle of the summer.

This tune, though, is most linked in my heart to *A Charlie Brown Christmas*. This is the carol the Peanuts gang sings at the end of the story, when they have learned their lesson that Christmas is not a commercial event. They finally know Christmas is the story of Christ coming to earth. "Hark," the perfect tune for them to sing.

I can hear the voice of Linus as he takes center stage. Charlie Brown has just asked, *"Does anyone know the true meaning of Christmas?"* Linus steps forward. He asks for the lights to dim. Then he tells the whole Nativity story from the Gospel of Luke, starting with the shepherds in the field, to the infant wrapped in swaddling clothes. Finally, he turns to Charlie Brown to say, *"And that's what Christmas is all about, Charlie Brown."* Simple. Perfect. Amazing.

It is amazing when you think of it, because it's a long Bible passage in the middle of a cartoon. Charles Schulz was bold when he insisted on putting this in the show. Nothing like this had ever hit the commercial airwaves before. It spoke so eloquently of the truth of the season. It was a testimony. And since 1963, the Peanuts special has been annually broadcast, reminding us of the true meaning of Christmas.

I doubt Charles Schulz thought of this as a bold move, putting a Bible passage in the middle of an animated show. For him I suspect it was the quiet conviction of knowing where the truth lay. The Christmas story is not about Santa coming down the chimney or picking the perfect gift. The Christmas story is the beginning of the greatest story ever told. And the most powerful place to find that is in the Bible.

There are all kinds of stories we pull out each year as treasured friends: *Miracle on 34th Street, White Christmas, It's a Wonderful Life, A Christmas Story,* and *How the Grinch Stole Christmas.* They all delight, and most have a message about the spirit of the season. But when you want to get to the heart of Christmas, Charlie Brown and Linus van Pelt will tell you all about it.

Thank You for the treasure of holiday entertainment
that brings joy to the season and reminds me of Your birth.
Amen

The Grinch

"Maybe Christmas," he thought, "doesn't come from a store.
"Maybe Christmas … perhaps … means a little bit more."
Dr. Seuss (Theodor Geisel)

How the Grinch Stole Christmas is my all-time favorite holiday show. I can hear Boris Karloff's voice narrating the story. And I love the Grinch's long-suffering dog, Max, and of course, "Little Cindy Lou Who who was no more than two." I am old enough to remember waiting for the show to come on television. The event was always heavily advertised. Back then, there was only one chance to watch it every year. It was on at a set time and set channel. You were either in front of the television or you missed it. I never missed it. Though one year I came very close.

I was in the children's choir at church. We sang in the annual Christmas pageant This particular year the performance was set for the same night *The Grinch* would be on television. I moaned about it all week. *We are never going to get home in time to see it. I am going to miss it!* But I had a commitment to sing at church. I even grumbled at rehearsal, though not so our director could hear. She was lovely, and I didn't want to disappoint her, but I still hated to miss the program.

Coordinating children in a live performance is tough, with the little ones not following directions, the shy ones not wanting to be onstage at all, and the loud ones making life backstage difficult. What a challenge. But our director had a keen idea. She brought a tiny television into the classroom where we were waiting backstage and at the appointed time she turned on *The Grinch!* Somehow, she timed our performance during a commercial break. I suspect it was a happy accident, but at the time I thought she was a genius.

Though we didn't see the whole show, our director made sure we saw most of it. I enjoyed singing in the choir very much, but will always remember that our director went out of her way to make sure we also got to see the once-a-year showing of *The Grinch.* She understood that the best way to love someone is to pay attention to what is important to them, even if it's a special television show. This Christmas, how can you love someone the way *they* need to be loved? It may be the best gift they receive all year.

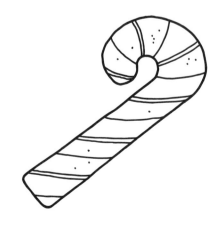

Maybe Christmas, perhaps, means
enjoying some joys from our past
as we celebrate the gift of our future.
Amen

It's Christmas Time in the City

Christmas Lights

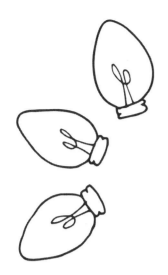
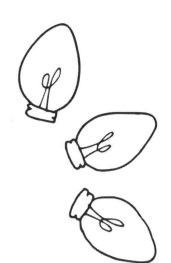

When Jesus spoke again to the people,
he said, "I am the light of the world.
Whoever follows me will never walk in darkness,
but will have the light of life."
John 8:12

The first year I had a place of my own, I got a full-size Christmas tree and dragged it up to my third-floor apartment. I wrestled it into a stand in the corner and started to decorate it. One string of lights was not enough. I went out and bought more. By the time I was done, my tree had three strings of lights, and twinkle lights outlined each of the three windows in my tiny apartment. I even strung lights in the kitchen. When a friend was visiting, he asked if the rest of the apartment building dimmed when I turned on all my lights. Ha-ha, very funny. I just really like Christmas lights.

Fast-forward a few years to home ownership. I still love lights, although it's harder to string them on the outside of a house. Every year I enlist my husband and son to help. They are not as excited about draining the power grid as I am. So, early in the season, our house has just a few lights along the eaves. And then, when I can't stand it, I put some on the bushes myself. I won't win any contests, but the glow really makes me smile. I always make sure to get out and enjoy the displays made by my creative and zealous neighbors. I never miss going to see the Mickey Mouse House, or the Christmas Town House or the Bear House. So fun. I'm sure there are great light shows in your neighborhood too.

There is one house around the corner that has a display that puts all my light-mania in perspective. They have a set of the old-fashioned plastic figures. They are about three to four feet high and they light up. While some people decorate their yards with Santa and his reindeer, or a gingerbread family, the family down the street has a shepherd, a sheep, three wise men, Mary, Joseph, and a cradle with baby Jesus. This is the holiday display that reminds me which light is most important: the Star in the East. A heavenly light announced the birth of our Lord. Fitting for the Light of the World to be heralded with the brightest and best Christmas light of all.

May the light of Christmas shine in my heart and be reflected in my life.
Amen

A Moment to Reflect

I wonder as I wander out under the sky,
How Jesus our Savior did come for to die,
For poor or'ny people like you and like I,
I wonder as I wander out under the sky.

John Jacob Niles

With all the busyness of Christmas, there seems little time for reflection. The to-do list of holiday cheer includes all kinds of good things: baking, shopping, partying, singing, wrapping. Many of our days are filled with fun, and the season rushes by. Suddenly it's January and we wonder how Christmas happened so fast.

Maybe you've found time to relax this season with some coloring. I hope so. But maybe there is no time during your holiday merrymaking to slow down and wonder about the season. It would be a mistake to never take a quiet moment to think about the gift of Christmas. You can think on it any time of year. I'm not trying to add to your holiday stress. If we don't allow ourselves a moment in December to reflect on the meaning of Christmas, though, we will almost certainly not allow ourselves that time in the middle of the year. There is always something filling our time and minds and days with obligations. We may never wonder as we wander through life.

Finding some time for quiet reflection and recharging feels essential to me. The words of this song seem to suggest the speaker is hiking. Taking a walk is one of my favorite ways to find a quiet moment. Out in nature there is space for my thoughts to roam as well as my body.

Just breathing in fresh air sets my spirit at peace. Then I can ponder a great question like, *Why did Jesus die for me?* Of course, I can't fathom why, yet thinking on it gives me an even deeper sense of awe and humility. When I open up room in my heart for this big question, it feels like I am giving God the opportunity to show me more of Himself. I question why and He seems to answer: *Because I love you; let Me show you how much.*

It may not be in December, but take some quiet time soon just to be in God's presence. He's waiting to tell you how much He loves you.

I can't unravel the mystery of Your love for me,
but tears prick my eyes when I get quiet and reflect on it.
Thank You so very much.
Amen

Lean in Close

He could have roared on top of a mountain,
but He whispered in the voice of a baby.
He could have ordered our obedience; instead He calls for our hearts.

Sheila Walsh

Shouting from a mountaintop may seem like the best way to capture someone's attention, but a whisper is what is saving the world. Screaming at someone is a violent way to interact. Whispering is intimate. You must get close to hear what is being said. God is so wise. He draws us close to give us His saving words of love.

It's tempting to yell when you want to be heard, especially if there is already a lot of noise in the environment. It seems necessary to raise your voice so people can hear what you have to say. We communicate with each other in many ways. Social media has exploded with options. Connect on Twitter, Tumblr, Instagram, Facebook, Pinterest, send an email or, heck, write an old-fashioned letter! We can get the word out and tell the world every detail. God had a better idea.

God chose the simplest way to reach our hearts, with love. The cry of a baby is what we are still listening to. The human touch is what draws us into the story and why we listen. It is personal. God came to earth as a baby. A baby can't even talk. The only message Jesus could bring was love. Babies just make you feel that "awwww" of love. Babies are helpless. You want to lean in close and cuddle. You want to whisper words of love to a newborn.

What a perfect way for God to capture our hearts: with love, with family, with a mother and a child. You are the child to whom God is whispering. We can hear God calling through the centuries to us individually: *"I love you."*

I suspect the season of Christmas is shouting at you right now. All kinds of things are screaming for your attention. There are distractions everywhere. But if you get quiet for just a moment, I think you might be able to hear a tiny baby crying in the midst of all the chaos. Jesus is whispering to your heart. Pick Him up, hold Him close, He has a beautiful message to share: *"I came for you. I love you."*

Lord, I am listening for the cry of Your heart to mine.
Amen

Peace

It came upon a midnight clear, that glorious song of old,
From angels bending near the earth, to touch their harps of gold:
"Peace on the earth, goodwill to men from heaven's all gracious King!"
The world in solemn stillness lay to hear the angels sing.

Edmund Hamilton Sears

When the headlines are screaming of terror and sadness, it's difficult to remember we have been wished peace from heaven above. We keep our heads down. We stay stuck. We harm each other in so many ways. From the global scale of terrorists to the personal abuses inside some homes, it can be difficult to remember peace. Yet *heaven's all-gracious King* is the One who sent us the message of *peace on earth, goodwill to men.*

Angel wings kissed Earth. A heavenly chorus sang to her. Peace was announced and given as a gift to the world. Though we have yet to enjoy peace throughout the world, we are still watched over by the King of the Universe. As crazy and mixed up as we have made life down here, He is still sending us the message that we matter to Him. He wants us to have peace. He is yearning for us to center our lives on Him and enjoy peace, one believer at a time.

No one person can individually make peace a global reality. Some problems are not for us to handle solo. We can, however, make our own corner of the world a little more peaceful. By concentrating on the individual part of Christmas, the part where you remember the gift of peace, of Christ softly coming into your heart. You. He came for you. What peace that brings! I am His!

The gift of peace to each individual is what we are all counting on to bring total peace to the world someday. For now you can enjoy peace in your heart, the calm truth that God is with you. So, sing of angels and be reminded that peace is a beautiful message of this season. And while we wait for it to come to the whole world, we can cherish it in our own hearts.

Peace on Earth seems so far out of reach, Father.
Calm my fears and bring me the peace of Your presence this Christmas.
Amen

Happy New Year

Christmas is not a myth, not a tradition, not a dream.
It is a glorious reality. It is a time of joy.
Bethlehem's manger crib became the link that bound a lost world to a loving God.
From that manger came a Man who not only taught us a new way of life,
but brought us into a new relationship with our Creator.
Christmas means that God is interested in the affairs of people,
that God loves us so much that He was willing to give His Son.

Billy Graham

It's time to take down the holiday decorations and pack them away for another year. Time to write thank-you notes for the lovely gifts we received and the parties we've attended. Time to look at the scale and see what all the holiday goodies have done to our waistline. Oh my. Time to start a happy New Year.

The reality of Christmas—a love from heaven so fierce we are still feeling it today—is what will make this a happy New Year. God is not stuck in the Christmas cradle. He's alive and well and working in every life. The joy of Christmas is not over.

As you tuck away all your holiday celebrations, it's a good time to think of how you can keep the reality of the Christmas season in your life. The birth of Christ has been uppermost in your mind for the past month. Why not continue that glorious thought into the New Year? Don't pack away all those positive thoughts of goodwill. Keep that part of the holiday active. Continue to celebrate the season in your heart.

I don't make resolutions every New Year. Sometimes I do and they are halfhearted and therefore doomed to fail, as you can imagine. This year, though, rather than a resolution to fix some trait I don't like about myself, I will try another approach. I resolve to keep the Christmas spirit in my heart. I'll let the Christ child rule in my life by daily invitation. To live as God wants me to be, I have to have His help. I can't do it on my own.

This will be a happy New Year, and I'll be eager to unpack all the Christmas decorations again at the end of the year and celebrate again with joy.

With Your help, Lord, my resolution is to live a more God-centered life this New Year.
Amen

Although it's been said many times many ways

A Christmas book has to be written in February, March, and April. So it can be produced during May, June, and July. So it can be printed, shipped, and stocked in October. It's a little nuts to work so far out of season. But having a great team makes it all go smoothly. No one ends up on the Naughty List. These are the nice people from Worthy Publishing I need to thank for helping me celebrate Christmas months in advance . . .

Nice

Pamela
Bart
Melissa
Cat
Leeanna
Byron
Marilyn
Betty
Debbie
Dale
Janet

INK

A Christmas Memory from the Author

To count down the days till Christmas, my mom made a red felt banner with two rows of tiny pockets across the bottom and a large green pine tree in the middle. Every morning from December first to the twenty-fourth, my sister and I would get up and rush to the Advent calendar hanging in the kitchen. There we would find a little ornament to pin on the felt tree. Then we'd dig into the pocket to find a piece of chocolate or a stick of gum or maybe a nickel.

When my son Zach was three, I wanted him to start enjoying this tradition. So I made a red felt banner with two rows of tiny pockets and a large green pine tree in the middle. Every morning from December first to the twenty-fourth, he pinned an ornament on the tree and ate a bit of chocolate. He liked it so much we did it every year. When he went off to college he wanted me to send the whole calendar to him filled and ready to go. Of course I was happy to oblige.

IF YOU ENJOYED THIS BOOK, WILL YOU CONSIDER SHARING THE MESSAGE WITH OTHERS?

Mention the book in a blog post or through Facebook, Twitter, Pinterest, or upload a picture through Instagram.

Recommend this book to those in your small group, book club, workplace, and classes.

Head over to facebook.com/LisaBogartAuthor, "LIKE" the page, and post a comment as to what you enjoyed the most.

Tweet "I recommend reading #DrawnIntoChristmas by Lisa Bogart // @worthypub"

Pick up a copy for someone you know who would be challenged and encouraged by this message.

Write a book review online.

WORTHY® PUBLISHING

Visit us at worthypublishing.com

twitter.com/worthypub   instagram.com/worthypub   pinterest.com/worthypub

facebook.com/worthypublishing   worthypub.tumblr.com   youtube.com/worthypublishing